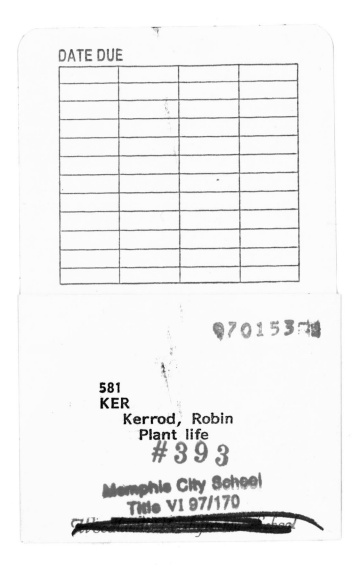

DATE DUE

LET'S INVESTIGATE SCIENCE
SCIENCE
Plant Life

LET'S INVESTIGATE SCIENCE
Plant Life

Robin Kerrod

Illustrated by Ted Evans

MARSHALL CAVENDISH
NEW YORK · LONDON · TORONTO · SYDNEY

Library Edition Published 1994

© Marshall Cavendish Corporation 1994

Published by Marshall Cavendish Corporation
2415 Jerusalem Avenue
PO Box 587
North Bellmore
New York 11710

Series created by Graham Beehag Book Design

Library of Congress Cataloging-in-Publication Data

Kerrod, Robin.
    Plant life / Robin Kerrod; llustrated by Ted Evans.
    p. cm. -- (Let's investigate science)
    Includes bibliographical references and index.
    ISBN 1-85435-627-5 ISBN 1-85435-688-7 (set)
    1. Plants--Juvenile literature. 2. Botany--Juvenile literature.
    [1. Plants. 2. Botany.] I. Evans, Ted ill. II. Title. III. Series: Kerrod, Robin.
    Let's investigate science.
    QK49.K45 1994   93-50186
    581--dc20   CIP
                                       AC

Printed and bound in Hong Kong.

Contents

Introduction

Plants make up one of the two main divisions, or kingdoms, of living things. Animals make up the other kingdom.

The first plants appeared on the Earth more than a billion years ago. They were simple, single-celled organisms called algae, some similar to the seaweeds we find on the seashore today. They too lived in the oceans.

Not until about 450 million years ago did plant life become firmly established on the land. And another 300 millions years went by before the first flowering plants appeared.

Today, the 300,000 or so known species of flowering plants that exist bring a blaze of color to our world. They bear blooms in all the colors of the rainbow. They grow on land and in the water, in tropical jungles and burning deserts, on bleak prairies and cold mountains.

Flowering plants range in size from a tiny, delicate, floating duckweed from Australia, which is less than one-fortieth of an inch (0.6 mm) across, to a gigantic coast redwood (sequoia) tree in California named for the National Geographic Society, which stands 374 feet (114 meters) tall.

In this book we investigate the biology of plants and look at the main plant groups and how they fit into the different environments we find on Earth.

For convenience, we consider algae and fungi as being different kinds of plants. But biologists now often classify these organisms in different kingdoms of living things.

You can check your answers to the questions featured throughout this book on pages 60-61.

◄ **Flowers beautify our world with colors of every hue. These flowers belong to a large family of plants that have flowers with petals arranged in a starlike shape. The name of the family, Asterales, means starlike.**

1
Plant Biology

◄ Flowers provide the means by which plants can reproduce, or produce more of their own kind. They are usually brightly colored and sweetly scented to attract the insects that will pollinate them.

Living things differ from non-living things in a number of ways. For example, they are able to feed, breathe, and grow. They are also able to reproduce, or produce offspring similar to themselves. Living things are also able to move in one way or another and are sensitive to their surroundings to a lesser or greater extent.

In this chapter, we look at the way plants feed, breathe, and reproduce. Plants not only eat food, they also make it. In this respect they differ from animals, which can't make food. Animals must eat plants or other animals that eat plants. So the ability of plants to make their own food is vital to all life on Earth.

Plants also differ from animals as far as movement and sensitivity to their surroundings are concerned. Most animals can move about bodily, whereas plants can't. They just move as they grow. Most animals have a number of specialized sense organs, such as eyes and ears, to sense their surroundings. Plants don't. But they do have limited senses that make their shoots grow toward the light and their roots grow downward because of gravity.

► The flower head of a teasel, a thistle-like plant. It bears hundreds of tiny flowers, called florets, each of which develops into a separate seed.

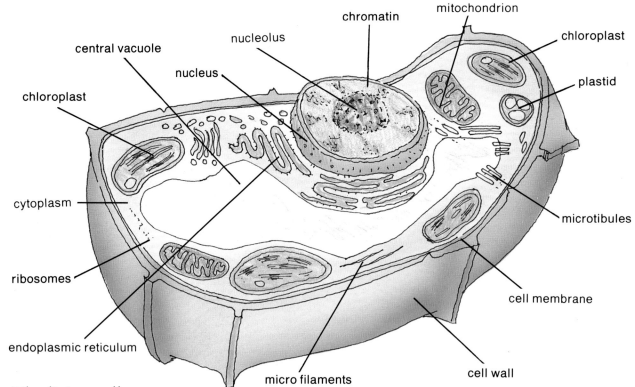

central vacuole

nucleolus

chromatin

mitochondrion

chloroplast

nucleus

plastid

chloroplast

cytoplasm

microtibules

ribosomes

cell membrane

endoplasmic reticulum

micro filaments

cell wall

10

The living cell

The basic unit of living things – plants or animals – is the cell. The cells in most living things are microscopic, measuring typically about 0.00025 inch (0.006 mm) across.

Q Assuming wood cells are of this size, figure out how many cells there are across the width of one of your wooden pencils.

Cell secrets

Plant cells are similar in many respects to animal cells. They consist of a mass of a jelly-like substance called cytoplasm, which is held within a kind of skin, or membrane. This allows certain materials to pass to and from the cell, while preventing others from doing so.

The most important part of the cell is the nucleus. This is the cell's communications and control center. It contains thread-like bodies called chromosomes, which carry thousands of units called genes. The genes hold the "plans" for the cell and indeed for the whole organism. The chromosomes are made up of a long complex molecule called DNA (see box opposite).

▲ The main features of a tropical plant cell, which is enclosed by a rigid cell wall of cellulose. Much of the cell is taken up by the vacuole, a space that holds the sugary plant sap. The chloroplasto are the parts containing green chlorophyll, which plays a vital part in photosynthesis, the plants food-making process.

Blueprint for life

The complex molecule that makes up a cell's chromosomes is deoxyribonucleic acid, or DNA. This molecule has a spiral structure, often referred to as a double helix. American biochemist James Watson and English biophysicist Francis Crick figured out the structure of DNA in the early 1950s and shared the 1962 Nobel prize for medicine for their work.

The two long spirals in the DNA molecule consist of long chains of alternating sugar and phosphate units. They are linked by pairs of chemicals called bases. Each gene in a chromosome is represented by a section of DNA containing a characteristic sequence of bases.

Other main structures in the cell include a network called the endoplasmic reticulum, which produces complex molecules such as proteins. Units called mitochondria produce the energy to keep the cell working.

Plant-cell differences

Both plant and animal cells have all the features just mentioned. But animals have some features plants lack. For one thing, each plant cell has a rigid cell wall around the membrane. This is made of a tough material called cellulose and gives plant parts their shape and helps them stay rigid.

Plant cells also contain a large "hole," called a vacuole. This contains plant sap, a sugary liquid. The cells in the green parts of plants also have units called chloroplasts. These contain the green pigment chlorophyll, which is essential to the plant's food-making process.

11

▶ This algae is a seaweed known as oar weed. Its wide fronds grow from a stalk that roots on the rocks.

Parts of a plant

Leaves
These form the plant's "food factory" and breathing organs. They make a sugary food by means of photosynthesis during daylight. They also give off water into the atmosphere in the form of vapor.

Flower
The showy part of the plant, which carries the reproductive organs and contains sweet nectar to attract the insects that help pollinate it.

Buds
These contain, the tightly curled leaves for next year's growth. They form during one growing season, but remain dormant during the winter, ready to start growing again in the spring.

Stem
This part typically supports the rest of the plant, thrusting up the leaves into the light. It also acts as a transportation system, carrying water up to the leaves and food from them to the other parts of the plant.

Roots
These absorb water and minerals from the soil. The other main purpose of the roots is to anchor the plant firmly in the ground.

Plant anatomy

The illustration opposite shows the main features of what we might call a typical plant. But really there is no such thing. Plants vary wildly in size and shape, as a walk through any forest will show.

The moss that grows underfoot, the wood anemones and bluebells that bloom in the spring, and the tall trees that tower above you are all quite different in their appearance and their way of life.

However, most plants have some kind of stems, roots, and leaves. There are two main kinds of stems. Trees have hard, strong woody stems. Lupins and delphiniums have soft, weak juicy stems, described as herbaceous.

Plants have two main kinds of roots. Dandelions have a single taproot; daisies have a spreading, fibrous root system. In the growing season the rate of root growth can be amazing. For example, grass roots can grow more than 2 inches (5 cm) in a day. Most water is absorbed into the roots through tiny root hairs. These have thin walls, that allow water to pass through readily.

Most plants have their roots buried in soil, but a few, called epiphytes or air plants, grow on trees and dangle their roots in the air. They absorb moisture from the air.

▲ A twig from a horse chestnut tree in winter. The buds are ready to shoot into growth as soon as the days lengthen and the weather becomes warmer in the spring. The twig bears the scars where last year's leaves separated and fell.

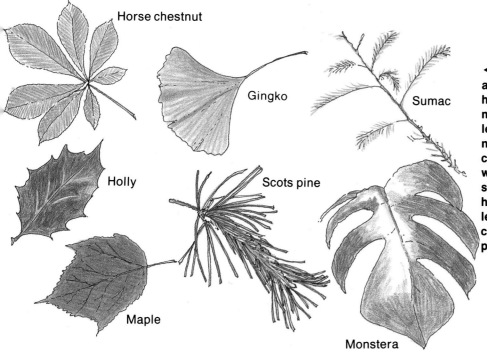

Horse chestnut

Gingko

Sumac

Holly

Scots pine

Maple

Monstera

◀ The leaves of plants come in all shapes and sizes. But they all have the same function – to make food for the plant. Certain leaf shapes have specific names. For example, the horse chestnut leaf is termed palmate, which means that it looks like spread out fingers on a hand. The maple has lobed leaves; the sumac has compound leaves. The Scots pine has needle-like leaves.

The miracle of photosynthesis

Here is an outline of the process by which a green plant makes its food. The name of the process, photosynthesis, means "making with light." It describes how a plant harnesses the energy in sunlight to bring about the food-making reactions that take place in its leaves.

14

Carbon dioxide
One of the two main raw materials (with water) for making food. The plant takes in this gas from the air through tiny pores on the underside of the leaves.

Oxygen
This gas is produced as a waste product during the food-making process and is given off through the pores on the underside of the leaves.

Green leaves
These contain chlorophyll, which captures energy from sunlight and makes it available for powering food production.

Transportation
Some tubes in the stem transport water up to the leaves from the roots. Others transport the food made in the leaves to other parts of the plant.

Water
One of the two main raw materials (with carbon dioxide) for making food. The plant takes in water through its roots.

Making food

As far as life on Earth is concerned, photosynthesis is one of the most important chemical reactions there is. It is the process by which green plants make food, a kind of sugar, in sunlight. A few plants, however, notably fungi, can't make their own food (see page 34).

Green plants make sugar by combining together the simplest of ingredients – carbon dioxide gas and water. The food-making process needs energy to work, and this energy comes from sunlight. The coloring matter that makes plants green, called chlorophyll, is responsible for trapping the energy in sunlight and making it available for the food-making reaction. An important waste product of the process is oxygen.

Food factories

In most plants, photosynthesis takes place mainly in the leaves, which are specially designed as "food factories." Most of the cells containing chlorophyll are located near the upper surface of the leaf. They are covered by a thin, transparent "skin."

Leaves take in the carbon dioxide they need from the air through tiny pores, called stomata, on their lower surface. The waste oxygen they produce also escapes from the leaves through the stomata.

The water the leaves need in order to make food is transported to them from the roots, which absorb moisture from the soil. Plants take in more water than they need, and the excess escapes from the leaves as vapor into the air through the stomata. In one day, a large tree can give off a ton or more of water vapor in this way

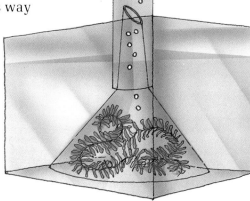

15

▲ **The mistletoe is a parasite that grows on the branches of trees, particularly apple and pear trees. It is not a complete parasite, though, because it makes its own food in its pale green leaves. It uses its host as an anchor and to provide water and minerals.**

INVESTIGATE

Take a large bunch of fresh water weed. (The weed sold for freshwater fish ponds – called Elodea – is ideal.) Place it in a bowl of water and put a clear plastic or glass funnel over it. Fill a test tube with water and upend it over the funnel, as shown in the picture.

On a sunny day, put the bowl in a light place. You should soon see tiny bubbles of gas coming from the weed. The gas will collect in the test tube, forcing out the water. When the tube is full of gas, remove it, keeping your thumb over the open end. Ask someone to light a candle for you and then blow it out. While the wick is still smoldering, plunge it into the test tube. What happens and why?

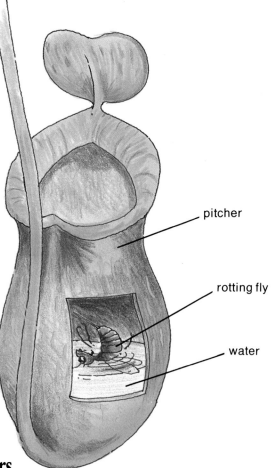

◄ A close-up of one of the pitchers of a pitcher plant, showing a fly trapped inside. Pitcher plants are natives of North America. The most common species, which has a purple flower, lives east of the Rockies in marshy ground.

pitcher

rotting fly

water

The meat-eaters

Most families of plants make their own food from carbon dioxide and water by photosynthesis. Some plant families, such as fungi and certain parasitic plants, rely on other plants for their food. And some even eat meat!

These meat-eating, or carnivorous, plants do not rely on the meat for all their food. Instead, they use it as a supplement to their diet. In particular, they obtain nitrogen from it, because they often live in poor soils where nitrogen is scarce.

Carnivorous plants are also called insectivorous plants because they obtain their meat by trapping insects.

Pitchers, bladders, and spring traps

Among carnivorous plants are the pitcher plant, bladderwort, and Venus flytrap. Pitcher plants are named for their leaves, which curl up to form the shape of a jug, or

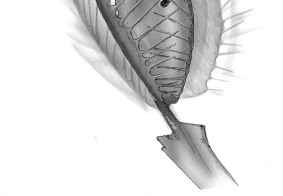

◀ The double leaf of the Venus flytrap carries sensitive hairs. When an insect touches them, the two halves spring shut. Venus flytraps are native to the southeastern North America. They are related to the sundew.

pitcher. The pitchers collect water. Insects attracted by honey on hairs fringing the top of the pitcher slip down the hairs into the water inside the plant and drown. Digestive juices in the water absorb nutrients from the insects as their bodies decay.

Bladderworts have many little bladders on their leaves, each with its mouth closed by a little trapdoor. When an insect touches sensitive hairs around the mouth, the bladder expands, opening the trapdoor and sucking the insect inside.

The Venus flytrap is probably the best known of the plant carnivores because it is now widely sold as a house plant. The plant has double "hinged" leaves. When an insect lands on a leaf, the two halves spring together and trap it.

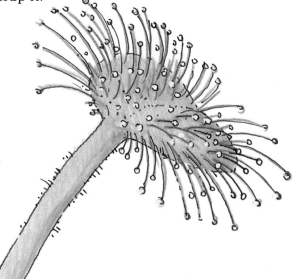

◀ The sundew has dew-like drops of sticky liquid on its leaves. When insects land on a leaf, they become stuck. The hairs on the leaf then bend over like tentacles to trap the victim.

Stages in the growth of a broad bean plant. No growth begins until the seed is planted in moist soil. The shoot that appears first travels downward to become a root. The next shoot travels upward to become the stem of the plant.

Q **1. Note that the root system becomes more extensive as the plant grows. Why is this important?**

18

Plant movement

Plants do not move around in the same way as animals, but they do move as they grow and in response to certain stimuli.

One of the stimuli that affects plant growth is gravity – the pull of the Earth. When you plant a bean seed, for example, it is the effect of gravity on the shoots emerging from the seed that makes one shoot bend upward to become the stem and the other downward to become the root. Bending movements like these are called tropisms.

Light also causes plants to move. Plant some corn seeds on damp blotting paper out in the open, and the seedlings will grow upright. Now place the plant on a window sill so that the seedlings get light from one direction only. You will find that they bend over toward the light. This is so their leaves can be exposed to as much sunlight as possible. This is another kind of tropism.

Q **2.** One of the tropisms mentioned above is called geotropism and the other is called phototropism. Which is which?

INVESTIGATE

Line a glass jar with blotting paper and stuff cotton cloth inside it. Place a bean seed between the paper and the glass. Thoroughly moisten the paper and cloth well and keep them moist. Stand the jar in a light place such as a window sill and look at the bean daily. See how it grows.

When the bean plant has sent out stem and root shoots, place the jar on its side, as shown in the picture. Observe what happens. Do the shoots keep on growing in the same directions as before? After a few days, stand the jar upright again. What happens?

bean

jar

cotton wool

blotting paper

19

Sensitive to touch

Some plants are sensitive to touch. Many climbers, such as the pea, have delicate tendrils that respond to touch. The tendrils grow rapidly when they touch something and coil tightly around it for support.

The most interesting touch-sensitive plant belongs to the mimosa family. We know it as the sensitive plant. When you touch its leaves, they curl up and appear to shrink away from you. No one knows why they do this.

Bindweed

▶ Honeysuckle and bindweed are among the most common climbing plants. The honeysuckle is widely planted in gardens for its sweet-smelling scent. It climbs in a clockwise direction. The bindweed, which climbs counterclockwise, is a troublesome weed in many gardens.

Honeysuckle

▲ You can see how this "spider plant" gets its name. It sends out runners all around it, which look rather like the legs of a spider. At the end of the runners new plants form.

Plant reproduction

All the familiar garden plants that produce flowers reproduce sexually. This means that they produce two kinds of cells, male and female. And in the reproduction process, male and female cells come together to form seeds, from which new plants will eventually grow (see page 22).

But many plants can reproduce without going through a sexual process. We say they reproduce asexually. Simple plants such as algae reproduce by simply splitting themselves in two. Yeast plants reproduce by budding, with a new plant growing as a bud on the old and then separating. Fungi and molds reproduce by means of tiny spores, from which new plants develop.

Vegetative reproduction

The strawberry plant, for example, can reproduce by sending out shoots called runners. Where the runners touch the soil, they develop roots and shoots and grow into other plants. This kind of asexual reproduction is an example of what is called vegetative reproduction.

Going underground

Other plants reproduce by sending out underground shoots, which we call rhizomes. Every so often they send up vertical shoots that develop into new plants.

Some plants reproduce from underground growths. A tulip, for example, grows from a bulb. As it grows, many little bulblets form around the old bulb, each of which will eventually grow into a mature plant.

Other plants reproduce by means of underground tubers, which are swollen root parts. The potato plant reproduces in this way. Each potato tuber will grow into another plant when planted.

Cutting and grafting

Gardeners often produce new plants asexually by taking cuttings. They cut a shoot from a mature plant and stick that in the soil. A new plant then grows from it.

Fruit and rose growers often produce new plants by grafting. They carefully cut a bud or a piece of stem from one plant and join it to another. The two plant parts eventually grow together as one. Grafting is usually carried out to produce plants with desired characteristics, such as disease resistance or dwarf tendencies.

21

▼ Vegetative reproduction below and above the ground, practiced by bracken and strawberry plants. Bracken can become a serious weed in farmland because it is difficult to get rid of every bit of the rhizome. Strawberry plants send out many runners, called stolons, that trail over the ground and root to form new plants.

Ⓠ Strawberry plants can reproduce in another way. How?

▲ This Bryophyllum plant produces tiny plantlets from notches at the edge of its leaves. Each will grow into a new plant. It is a common house plant, sometimes called the life plant. It is a native of Africa.

Sexual reproduction

The most common way plants multiply is by sexual reproduction. All flowering plants reproduce sexually. Their sex organs are contained in the flower. In brief, this is what happens.

The male organs in the flower produce sex cells in the form of a powdery dust known as pollen. The pollen is carried in one way or another to the flower of another plant of the same species. Once there, the pollen grains, which you remember are male cells, combine with the second plant's female, or egg, cells. These egg cells now develop into seeds, from which new plants can eventually grow.

The diagram below shows the main features of a flower. The pistils (carpels) form the female part. They receive pollen which is channeled down to the egg cells in the ovary. The stamens are the male parts, which produce the pollen.

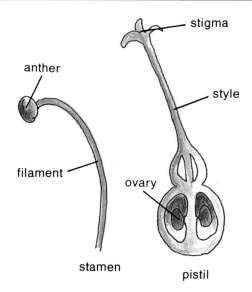

▲ **Details of the male and female parts of a flower – the stamen and the pistil. The pollen is contained in a tiny sac in the anther. The sticky style picks up pollen carried to it from other flowers.**

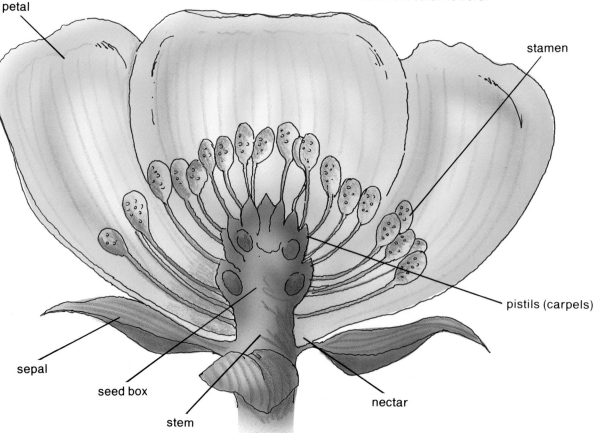

◀ The showy flower of the hibiscus known as the Rose of China. It thrives in tropical and subtropical regions of the world, and is a popular house plant elsewhere.

▼ The spikes of this plantain are actually flowers. They are not showy like the flower in the picture on the left, because they do not need to attract insects.

Ⓠ How do you think they scatter their pollen?

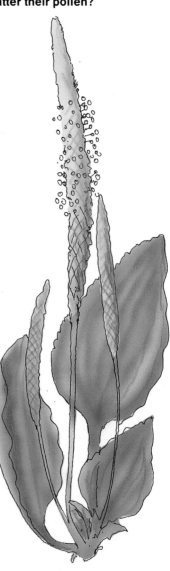

Conifer cones

Conifers also produce seeds by sexual reproduction. But unlike the flowering plants, conifer seeds are "naked" – they have no protective covering.

A conifer tree produces two kinds of cones, male and female. The scales of the male cones carry pollen. In spring, the cones open slightly. The male cones release their pollen into the air, and it enters the female cones. The male cones then wither and drop from the tree. The female cones close up. Inside, the pollen fertilizes the egg cells, which develop into hard winged seeds.

Moss spores

Mosses produce spores as part of their life cycle the way fungi do. However, in another part of their life cycle, mosses grow male and female parts and produce male and female sex cells. In wet weather, when the plant is covered with moisture, the male parts release tiny cells, which swim to the female parts and fertilize the egg cells. From these grow capsules containing spores, which scatter and grow into new plants.

Pollination

The transfer of pollen from the stamens of one flower to the pistils of another is called pollination. Pollination is necessary to bring about the fertilization of the egg cells in the pistils. Only then can the flower produce seeds.

Some flowers are self-pollinated. This means that they can be fertilized by their own pollen. Most flowers, however, are cross-pollinated. This means that they are fertilized only when they receive pollen from other flowers of the same kind.

24

Blowing in the wind

Some plants rely on the wind to carry pollen from flower to flower. Many trees and shrubs, as well as grasses, corn, and other cereal crops, use wind pollination.

If you shake the flower heads of grasses in the spring, the pollen showers out. This is typical of plants that rely on wind pollination – they produce an abundance of pollen to ensure that at least some of it can reach other plants of the same kind.

Q 1. Grass pollen not only fertilizes grass, it also affects people. How?

▲ The hazel, or cobnut, tree has separate male and female flowers. The female flowers are difficult to see, looking somewhat like buds. The long catkins on the tree are the male flowers.

Q 2. How can we tell that the catkins are the male flowers?

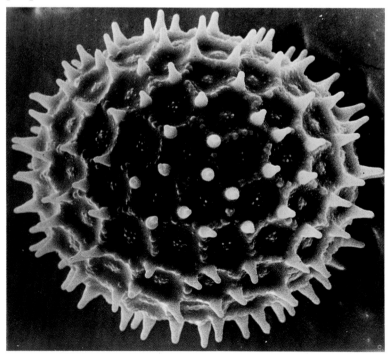

◀ A highly magnified photograph of a pollen grain, taken with a scanning electron microscope. It comes from the common morning glory plant and is about 1,200 times bigger than life-size. Other plants produce pollen with very different shapes.

The bees and the birds

Wind pollination is sort of a hit or miss method of fertilizing flowers. So most flowering plants have a more reliable method of pollination. They rely on insects, and sometimes birds and bats, to carry pollen.

Most flowers that rely on insects to pollinate them have showy petals and a scent and produce sugary nectar. This serves to attract insects to them. As the insects probe for the nectar, they get dusted with pollen from the stamens, which they then carry to another flower. There, they brush against the pistils, and pollen is transferred.

▶ A close-up picture of a honey-bee, one of the most useful pollinators of flowering plants. The bee not only carries pollen from flower to flower, it also collects pollen in little "baskets" on its hind legs and takes it back to the hive to be used as food.

Q Are the bees that collect pollen males or females?

▲ Butterflies are among the many insects that pollinate flowering plants. They thrust their long proboscis into the flower head to feed on the nectar the flower produces.

Seeds and fruits

Seeds start to form in a flower when the egg cells in its ovary are fertilized. The process of fertilization begins when pollen settles on a stigma and sends down a tube to the ovary. Male cells then travel down the tube and combine with, or fertilize, the egg cells.

The fertilized egg cells develop into seeds. At the same time, the structures around them change, too. They become the fruit. The fruit may be fleshy and moist, as in apples, or soft and juicy, as in oranges. Some trees and shrubs produce fruit in the form of nuts. The seed is contained in a tough shell and is called the kernel.

26

poppy seed head

Scattering the seeds

When the seeds and fruits of plants are ripe, they separate and fall to the ground. There, when conditions are right, they will germinate, or begin to grow. In time, they will develop into a mature plant, which will flower and seed in turn.

sycamore

lupin seed pods

▲ **Different methods of seed dispersal.**
The poppy produces tiny, light seeds, which blow away readily on the wind. The sycamore tree produces seeds with little wings attached so that they can glide through the air like a helicopter. Lupin seeds are flung out when their pods burst. Birds spread blackberry seeds. Squirrels help spread nuts by burying them. They eat some, but enough remain to grow into new plants.

However, if the seeds simply fell beneath the parent plant and grew there, they would become overcrowded and soon exhaust the nutrients in the soil. So plants use a number of methods of scattering their seeds over as wide an area as possible.

Many plants rely on the wind to scatter their seeds. Dandelions and thistles produce seeds with tiny "parachutes" attached, which blow away with the wind. Gorse and vetch produce seeds in pods, which suddenly burst and hurl the seeds away.

Plants that bear juicy fruits rely on animals, particularly birds, to spread their seeds. Birds feasting on fruits such as blackberries take in the tiny seeds they contain. Then they fly away. Eventually, the seeds pass through the birds and are deposited with their droppings.

Furry animals help distribute the seeds of some plants, including the buffalo burr. They produce burrs, or seeds covered by tiny hooks that catch in the animal's fur and can be carried for miles before they come off.

▼ A selection of luscious fruits from around the world. Thanks to speedy refrigerated transportation, they can now be enjoyed in countries far removed from where they are cultivated. The fruits in the picture include mango, lychee, kiwi fruit, passion fruit, sharon fruit, physalis or cape gooseberry, and kumquat.

28

◄ The vicious prickles on a blackberry stem. Their hook-like shape snags into flesh easily, causing painful wounds. But the main purpose of the prickles is to help the plant climb through other vegetation and not, as you might be tempted to think, to seek revenge on those trying to pick its fruit!

▼ The common stinging nettle is covered with hairs with tips like a hypodermic needle. They dig into the skin and inject their irritating poison.

Ⓠ The drab-colored, dangling clusters you see in the picture are the flowers of the plant. How do you think these flowers are pollinated?

Plant defenses

If you have picked blackberries or accidentally walked bare-legged through a clump of nettles, you will have experienced two ways in which plants protect themselves.

Blackberry bushes grow long stems covered with vicious curved prickles that tear at the flesh. This discourages animals from trampling or eating them. However, the main function of the prickles is to help the plant climb through other vegetation. Roses have the same kind of prickles.

We often call such prickles "thorns." But to be strictly accurate, thorns are dwarf branches. The prickles on blackberry and rose bushes, however, grow out of the skin. The hawthorn and blackthorn bear true thorns. Other plants have prickles called spines, which are modified leaves, or grow them on the leaves, as in thistles.

► A barrel cactus growing in the Arizona Desert. It is covered with needle-sharp stiff spines. The remains of its flowers can be seen at the top.

▼ This plant has nettle-like leaves, but they do not sting. That is why the plant is called a dead-nettle. The fact that it has nettle-like leaves may help protect it.

Q In the animal world there are many examples of one kind of species gaining protection by resembling another. What is this characteristic called?

Plants with a sting

Many plants have their stems and leaves covered with some kind of hair. This covering may help insulate the plant, keeping it warm in a cold climate and cool in a hot climate. Or it may help reduce water loss in a dry climate.

But in some plants the hairs act as protection. Many members of the nettle family, for example, are covered with stiff hairs containing a toxic liquid. The tip of the hairs is sharp and brittle and penetrates the skin like a hypodermic needle. Under the skin, it breaks off and releases the liquid, which causes a stinging sensation.

The stings from most nettles usually remain painful for only an hour or so and are not serious. Stings from the tree nettle of Australia, however, are vicious and agonizingly painful. Their effects can last for months.

The poison ivy protects itself in another way, by secreting an oily liquid from its leaves. This liquid irritates the skin and makes it blister.

2
Plant Groups

◀ Delicate blooms of a swamp lily, photographed in the Florida Everglades. The lily is one of the largest families of flowering plants, which also includes a wide variety of plant species such as the leek, the lily of the valley, and the tulip.

We know there are more than 350,000 different kinds, or species, of plants in the world. They vary widely in their appearance, where they live , how they reproduce, and so on.

The seaweed that grows on rocks at the seashore is quite different from the moss that grows on the ground in damp places, the fungi that grow on decaying tree stumps, the colorful wild flowers that bloom on the prairie, and the huge conifer trees that thrust majestically hundreds of feet into the sky.

Each of the kinds of plants mentioned above – seaweed, moss, fungi, flowers, and conifers – belongs to a fundamentally different plant group. In this chapter, we look at examples of plants within these groups. But we begin, on the next page, with a kind of plant-group "family tree."

▶ Despite constant battering by the waves, a mat of algae clings tenaciously to a rock off the Pacific coast of California. Algae are among the most primitive of all plants.

The plant family tree

Here is one way in which we can picture the plant kingdom, as a kind of family tree. It brings together the main and distinctly different groups of plants and provides a basis for plant classification. As mentioned earlier, algae and fungi are now often classified in different kingdoms.

Botanists classify plants by arranging them into groups according to their characteristics. They do this on several levels, beginning with a broad group, in which the plants are only distantly related. The broad group is then broken down into subgroups, in which the plants have more characteristics in common. Each subgroup is in turn broken down into further subgroups, in which the plants are even more closely related.

Scientists have special names for the various groups and subgroups in the classification of the plant kingdom. The first broad group is "division." The next is "class," followed by "subclass," "order," "family," "genus," and "species."

For example, botanists classify a common wild flower, the oxeye daisy or white daisy, in the following way:

Division: Spermaphyta
Class: Angiospermae
Subclass: Dicotyledonae
Order: Asterales
Family: Compositae
Genus: Chrysanthemum
Species: leucanthemum

Note that the classification names are in Latin. This follows the lead of the person who pioneered classification in the 1700s. He was the Swedish biologist Carl Linne, who preferred to be called by his Latinized name, Carolus Linnaeus.

Botanists generally refer to plants by their Latin names, based on their classification. They would refer to this daisy, for example, as Chrysanthemum leucanthemum.

Botanists use Latin names rather than common names, because the same plant can be called different names in different countries. The plant Arum maculatum, for example, may be called lords-and-ladies, cuckoo pint, and wake robin.

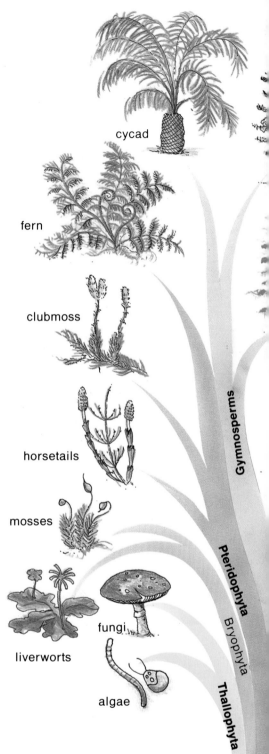

cycad

fern

clubmoss

horsetails

mosses

liverworts

fungi

algae

Gymnosperms

Pteridophyta

Bryophyta

Thallophyta

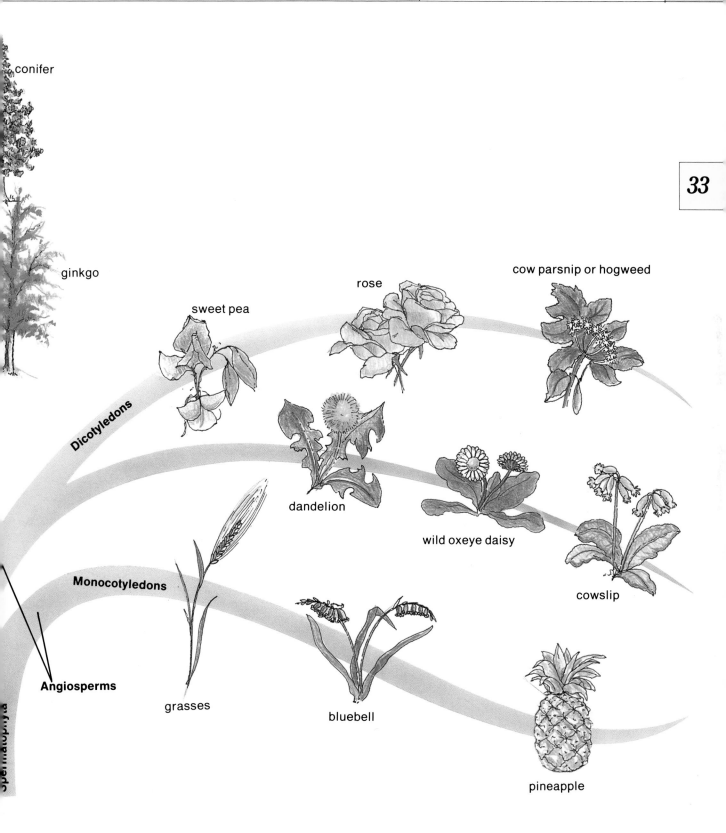

conifer

ginkgo

sweet pea

rose

cow parsnip or hogweed

Dicotyledons

dandelion

wild oxeye daisy

cowslip

Monocotyledons

grasses

bluebell

Angiosperms

pineapple

▶ **This alga is Pandorina. It is a colonial type, made up of several plants joined together.**

▼ **Spirogyra is a common pond weed. It is named for its spiral structure.**

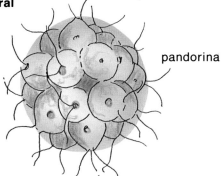

pandorina

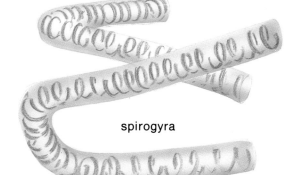

spirogyra

Primitive plants

The simplest plants of all are the algae. They belong, with fungi, to the plant division Thallophyta. Unlike fungi, however, all algae contain chlorophyll and can therefore make their own food. Nearly all of them live in the water, both in fresh water and in the oceans.

In ponds

Many algae are microscopic and are made up of a single cell. One of the most common is the fresh-water alga Chlamydomonas. Like some other algae, it possesses two whip-like threads, called flagella, which it lashes around so it can swim.

Another common alga is Spirogyra, which forms into dense mats that clog many ponds in the summer.

In the sea

There are also microscopic algae in the sea, which form part of the drifting plankton that many fish and whales live on.

But the most obvious algae in the sea are the seaweeds. They include kelp, the largest form of which, the Pacific giant kelp, can grow as much as 18 inches (45 cm) in a day and reach up to 215 feet (65 meters) in length!

Q **1.** Seaweeds grow only in relatively shallow coastal waters. Why can't they grow in the ocean depths?

▼ **This seaweed is called bladder wrack. Its air-filled bladders help it float when the tide comes in.**

Q **2. What would be the advantage of this?**

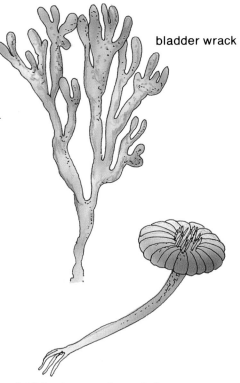

bladder wrack

▲ **This strange-shaped alga, Acetabularia, is popularly called mermaid's wine glass. As long as your finger, it consists of a single cell.**

INVESTIGATE

2. Take a large open mushroom and carefully remove its stalk. Place it, gills-down, on a sheet of white paper. Cover it with a bowl and leave it for about a week.

1. Mushrooms produce their spores from the dark brown gills that grow under the cap. The spores are too tiny to see on the plant, but you can make them visible by making a spore print.

3. After that time, remove the bowl and carefully lift up the mushroom. You should find a pattern made by the spores falling from the mushroom.

Ferns, mosses, and liverworts

These are much more advanced plants than the algae and reproduce by means of spores. They live mostly in damp places.

The ferns are one of the oldest plant groups, dating back hundreds of millions of years. At that time, great forests of ferns more than 100 feet (30 meters) tall grew in many parts of the world.

Q 1. Today, we find plenty of evidence of these great forests. What is this evidence?

The fungi

The mushrooms we eat and the toadstools we find in the woods and fields are examples of fungi (singular, fungus). They, too, reproduce by means of spores. The molds that grow on bread, cheese, and other foods left out in the air are also simple fungi. So are yeasts.

Q 2. Mushrooms are white and they can grow in the dark. What does this tell us about them?

▼ Lichen growing on a rock. There are about 15,000 species of lichen, some of which grow in the coldest habitats, including Antarctica. The lichen is a strange "combination" plant, consisting of an alga and a fungus living intimately together. Neither could exist without the other.

The cone-bearers

It was a great evolutionary step in the plant kingdom when plants began to produce seeds rather than spores. Seeds have three things going for them. They have the beginnings of a new plant (embryo), contain the food to nourish it when it begins to grow, and have an outer covering to protect it.

Two main groups of seed-producers exist today, the conifers and the flowering plants. The conifers, or cone-bearers, produce their seeds in cones. They are known as gymnosperms ("naked seeds") because their seeds are not enclosed in fruits. In all, there are over 500 species of conifers.

The biggest region of conifer forest occupies a broad belt across northern North America, Europe, and Asia. It is made up of species such as pines, firs, and spruces.

▲ The Monterey pine is a native of the coastal region of Monterey, California, where it is found clinging precariously to the rocks. It grows only to about 65 feet (20 meters) tall. The biggest populations of Monterey pines are now found in New Zealand and elsewhere in the Southern Hemisphere, where they are planted for timber and where they grow much taller.

Cone of the Monterey pine.

The western hemlock is a native of North America, where it is a valuable timber tree.

The cones of the Bhutan pine, a native of the Himalayas, grow up to 1 foot (30 cm) long.

The Douglas fir is one of the tallest conifers, capable of reaching a height of more than 295 feet (90 meters). It is found in abundance in the Rocky Mountains.

These trees are similar in that their leaves are narrow and sharp, like needles, and they are evergreen. The needle-like leaves are better than broad ones at reducing heat loss, which is important in the long, cold northern winters. Leaves stay on the trees the whole year and do not drop in the fall like the leaves of deciduous trees. A few conifers, however, are deciduous, including the larch and some cypresses.

Conifers grow, too, in warm parts of the world. Their needle-like leaves catch the sun less than broad-leaved trees do, and also minimize the loss of water.

► A dazzling display put on by bougainvillea, a climbing plant that thrives in warm climates. It is a native of South America, but is now widely planted in tropical and subtropical regions throughout the world.

Lily of the Valley

Hyacinth

Thistle

Wild parsnip

▲ Some plants produce a single flower on a stem; others produce several. All the flowers together are called an inflorescence. The multiple flowers on a plant may be carried in a variety of different ways.

Flowering plants

The flowering plants form the largest group within the plant kingdom. They occupy the class Angiosperma, and are known as angiosperms. The word angiosperma means "enclosed seeds." This refers to the fact that the seeds of flowering plants develope within a protective seed coat that becomes a fruit.

The flowers of flowering plants vary widely, not only in color but also in form. Some flowers, such as roses, are classed as complete flowers because they have all the parts of a typical flower – sepals, petals, stamens, and pistils. Incomplete flowers lack one or more of these parts.

The marsh marigold, for example, has no petals. Instead its large yellow sepals form the flower. All the flowers on a marrow plant look similar, but some only have stamens, and others only pistils. They are in fact separate male and female flowers. In some trees, such as the holly, male and female flowers grow on separate trees.

Year by year

Many flowering plants go through their whole life cycle of germinating, growing, flowering, and seeding in just one growing season. Then they die. They are known as annuals. Cornflowers and marigolds are examples.

Some plants take two growing seasons to mature. They are known as biennials. Foxgloves and hollyhocks are examples.

Other plants, once they have grown into mature plants, remain alive indefinitely, flowering and producing seeds every year. Called perennials, they include daisies, primroses, and violets. All plants that grow from bulbs, such as daffodils and tulips, are perennials.

Q What other group of large flowering plants are perennials?

▲ Orchids are among the most attractive plants on Earth. Their blooms can be stunning, both in color and in form. All blooms have six petals, one of them has a special shape and is called the lip. It has markings to guide insects to the nectar inside the flower.

▼ Many of the 1,000 or so species of cacti have very attractive flowers. They come as a surprise on what are otherwise plain plants.

◄ A magnolia tree in full bloom in New England. The large cup-like flowers are fragrant and colored pink and white.

Flowering trees

There is a world of difference between a horse chestnut and a lupin. The one is a huge tree growing up to 110 feet (35 meters) tall, while the other is a herbaceous plant that reaches up to about 3 feet (1 meter). But they are both flowering plants. Every year the chestnut produces spiky flowers that are fertilized by pollen and then form seeds. These seeds are contained in a prickly case.

Trees are, in fact, the largest plants in existence. Yet they behave like and have the same structure as most small plants. The major difference is that they develop a sturdy stem, the trunk, which gives them the support they need to stay upright over many years.

The trunk is made up of woody tissue, but it is not the same all the way through. On the outside is the bark, which provides a protective covering for the trunk as a whole, and in particular for a layer of living cells underneath it, called the cambium.

The cambium is really the most important part of the whole tree. Inside the tree in the growing season, it grows new tissue called xylem, which adds to the trunk's girth. The xylem contains tubes that carry water up to the leaves from the roots. The part of the trunk that has water-carrying tubes is called the sapwood. The oldest wood at the center of the tree, the heartwood, no longer carries water.

On the outside of the cambium, a layer of cells called phloem carries food made by the leaves to other parts of the tree.

◀ Like other oaks, the red oak bears acorns in neat cups.

▲ The tulip tree is named for its tulip-like blooms. It is a native of eastern North America, where it is the tallest of the broad-leaved trees. It can reach a height of 190 feet (58 meters) under favorable conditions.

◀ Blooms of the flowering dogwood. The white "petals" are not petals at all; they are leafy structures called bracts. The true flowers are small and located in the center.

▲ Several trees have a drooping, or "weeping" habit, including this weeping willow.

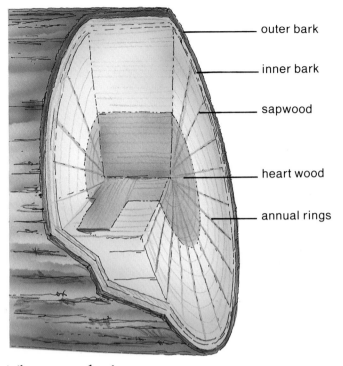

— outer bark

— inner bark

— sapwood

— heart wood

— annual rings

◄ A cross-section of a tree trunk, showing its structure. The sapwood carries water up to the leaves; the harder heartwood no longer does so. The cambium is the most important part of the tree, that which produces new wood.

42

The growth rings

Every year the trunk of a tree gets thicker. This is because during the year a layer of new wood tissue has been added to it. This new wood is produced by the cambium.

In the spring, when the tree is growing fastest, the cambium produces tissue with large water-carrying tubes, allowing the flow of plenty of water to the leaves. As growth slows down in the fall, the cambium grows tissue with progressively narrower tubes, and in winter none at all. The next spring sees the cambium producing large-tube tissues once more.

When you look at the cross-section of a cut-down tree trunk, you can easily see the boundaries between the fall and spring tissues. They appear as concentric rings, which we call growth rings or annual rings.

By counting the number of rings, you can figure out the age of the tree. By carefully examining the relative sizes and structure of the rings, you can get an idea of the growing conditions in each year of its life. Scientists use this principle to study past climates, working with aged trees like the bristlecone pines of California, which can be 4,000 years old or more. The method of studying tree rings in this way is known as dendrochronology.

▲ A giant sequoia, or redwood tree in the Sequoia National Park in the Sierra Nevada Range in California. Some trees are big enough to have a road running through them.

Scale: 1mm = 20 years

tree starts
to grow
AD 400

A   C   E   G   I   K

B   D   F   H   J   L   present

▼ **Some of the giant sequoias in California are believed to be thousands of years old. When they are felled, we can calculate their great age by counting their annual rings. We could mark significant dates in history on them, as shown here.**

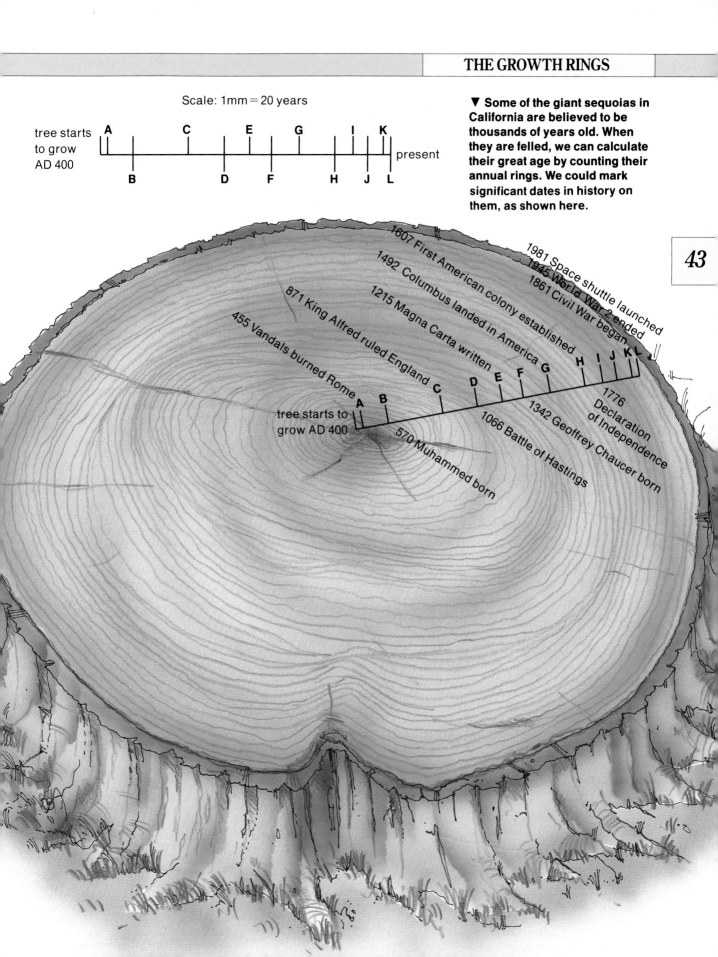

1981 Space shuttle launched
1945 World War 2 ended
1861 Civil War began
1807 First American colony established
1492 Columbus landed in America
1215 Magna Carta written
871 King Alfred ruled England
455 Vandals burned Rome
tree starts to grow AD 400
570 Muhammed born
1066 Battle of Hastings
1342 Geoffrey Chaucer born
1776 Declaration of Independence

A B C D E F G H I J K L

The grasses

As far as many animals, including human beings, are concerned, the most important family of plants is one of the simplest. It is the grass family, which contains more than 2,000 different species.

Ordinary grass covers much of the world's land, from the prairies of North America to the savanna of Africa. It provides food for countless species of grazing animals – such as rabbits, rhinoceroses, horses, hippopotamuses, and so forth.

Forage and cereals

As far as human beings are concerned, grass is important as a major forage crop, one grown to feed livestock such as cattle and sheep. Even more important are the different kinds of grasses that we know as cereals, such as wheat, corn, rice, barley, oats, and rye.

▼ Grass provides the basic diet for grazing animals, such as dairy cattle. Cattle have a many-chambered stomach in which the grass is broken down in stages as it passes from chamber to chamber. The first chamber is called the rumen, and cattle are called ruminants.

The cereals have been developed over the past 10,000 years by selective breeding from wild grasses. They are now produced in huge quantities, especially on the vast prairie regions of North America and Russia. The United States alone produces some 80 million tons (74 million tonnes) of wheat and 220 million tons (200 million tonnes) of corn each year.

Another kind of grass invaluable to humans is one of the tallest – sugar cane. It can grow more than 15 feet (4.5 meters) tall and has stems about 2 inches (5 cm) across.

Life style

Grasses belong to one of the two branches of flowering plants, the monocotyledons. These are narrow-leaved plants whose seeds have one seed leaf.

Grasses are flowering plants, but their flowers are dull and inconspicuous. They form on spikes and have neither colorful petals nor a scent. They are pollinated by the wind.

▲ Bamboo is another member of the grass family, one that can grow to enormous heights – up to 120 feet (36 meters). The plant thrives best in warm climates and grows in profusion in tropical Asia. The young shoots of the bamboo form an important part of the diet in the Far East.

◄ Hundreds of thousands of acres of sawgrass cover the Everglades in Florida. This unique wetland area is often called the "river of grass." Sawgrass is so called because its edges are covered with tiny jagged teeth.

3
Plants in Their Habitats

◀ **Bluebells, or wild hyacinths, carpet a wood in springtime. They grow and flower before all the leaves appear on the trees when plenty of sunlight can still reach them.**

▶ **A flower blooms in the arid, stony Arizona Desert, shortly after a rain shower. Desert plants are well adapted to their habitat. They can remain dormant for a very long time until the rain comes. Then they burst into life, flower, and seed in just a few weeks.**

Every species of plant lives best in certain conditions. The showy poinciana tree of Hawaii, with its spectacular scarlet blooms, thrives in the warmth and moisture of the tropics. It could not live in the warm desert regions of Arizona because it is too dry there. It also could not live in the moist coastal regions of Washington State because of the cold.

The Saguaro cactus, however, thrives in the Arizona deserts, and the giant redwood thrives in Washington State. These plants are suited to the particular conditions in their habitats.

The most important factor that determines a habitat is the climate – especially the temperature and the amount of rainfall. In this chapter we will see how particular plants are adapted to living in various habitats.

In hot places

Plants grow in the greatest profusion in the equatorial regions of the world, where there is warmth and constant moisture. Temperatures average 70-80°F (21-28°C) all year round, and rain falls almost every day. Frosts that might check plant growth are unheard of.

It is in such regions that the rain forests grow. Broad-leaved evergreens such as mahogany and teak are the most common trees. Their upper branches and leaves form a dense layer called the canopy, averaging some 60-70 feet (18-21 meters) high. This layer blots out most of the sunlight, making the forest floor dark. Fungi abound there, living on the decaying vegetation, but flowering plants are scarce.

Q Why are fungi common but flowering plants scarce on the forest floor?

Up in the air

Flowers can be found in the forests, but high up in the trees. They grow on the branches and in crevices in the bark. They use the trees they live on simply as support, making their own food by photosynthesis and obtaining moisture directly from the very humid air. The most spectacular of these air plants, or epiphytes, are the orchids.

Other plants, known as bromeliads, form "tanks" out of overlapping leaf bases. These can hold several quarts of water, which provide a home for frogs and tadpoles, and even crabs!

▲ This is a moth orchid, named for its moth-like flowers. It grows from seeds that lodge in the bark of trees and germinates there. It sends out roots that dangle in the air. They take in water directly from the damp atmosphere.

◄ Fruits ripening on a lemon tree, an evergreen with glossy leaves. A native of south-east Asia, it is now grown commercially in many other tropical and subtropical regions, including southern California.

In the desert

In the deserts of the world, there is plenty of heat but precious little water. So the plants that survive there have to adapt to these conditions. The typical desert plant is the cactus, common throughout the searing hot deserts in the United States and Mexico.

▼ The Saguaro cactus of the Arizona Desert. Also called the giant cactus, it can reach a height of 40 feet (12 meters) or more. It can live for up to 200 years.

Cacti are notable for their tough, fleshy stems, which are covered in spines. These stems are filled with a sponge-like tissue that is able to hold water, so that the plant can soak up any moisture that appears. The plants have no real leaves, and photosynthesis therefore takes place in the stems.

▼ The Joshua tree, which has given its name to the desert region that forms the Joshua Tree National Monument in southern California.

In cold places

Just as the searing heat of desert climates provides a challenge to plant life, so does the freezing cold of the far northern and far southern latitudes of the world.

In the Northern Hemisphere, the climate becomes harsh for plant life in the region occupied by the northern, or boreal, forests. They stretch in a great belt over the north of North America, Europe, and Asia.

A few species of broad-leaved, deciduous trees are found in the forests, including birch, aspen, and willow. But the dominant kind of tree is the evergreen conifer. It boasts several features that illustrate ways in which plants adapt to the cold.

It has narrow, needle-like leaves, because they don't lose heat as quickly as the broad leaves. They also tend to trap pockets of air between them, which gives added protection and reduces water loss.

The fact that the trees are evergreen is also an advantage. With leaves already in place, the tree can burst quickly into growth the moment temperatures start to rise in the spring. It does not have to wait for buds to develop, as happens with deciduous trees.

50

◄ The silver birch is a graceful tree with a sivery-white bark. It is very hardy and grows in the far north.

► The Norway spruce is a common tree in the northern forest belt. A typical conifer, it bears its seeds in cones, has needle-like leaves, and has a conical shape.

◄ Evergreen conifer forests thrive in cool climates. They are widely planted for their softwood timber, used in house-building and as raw material for making paper. They mature much quicker than the deciduous hardwoods, such as oak.

On the tundra

North of the great northern forest belt is the region known as the tundra. Most of it lies within the Arctic Circle, and the climate is very harsh indeed.

The ground is frozen and snow-covered during the very long winter, which lasts most of the year. Then, temperatures plummet to −60°F (−50°C) and below. The other three seasons are squeezed into about three months, and the growing season for plants is even shorter – a matter of perhaps 6-8 weeks. During this time, they have to make new growth, produce flowers, and form ripe seeds.

Most of the plants that live on the tundra are perennials that burst into growth the instant the snows melt, producing blooms within a few days and seeds as soon as four weeks later. Among the plants are strawberries, sedges, and cottongrass. These plants are low-growing with a compact habit, which helps protect them from the biting winds. Large trees are absent on the tundra, but dwarf willows and dwarf birches grow in places. Mosses and lichens are also widely found, even in the most exposed and rockiest places.

51

▼ Caribou move on to the North American tundra as the spring melts the winter snow. They graze on the coarse grasses that blanket the landscape. The surface is boggy because the meltwater can't drain away through the still-frozen soil.

◀ This tropical flower of the lily family grows at the edge of a lake on the island of Bali, Indonesia, just a few degrees south of the Equator. There, the ground and the air are always moist.

In watery places

There are many kinds of watery places, or wetlands, on Earth – including the margins of stagnant ponds and flowing rivers, bogs and swamps, and mudflats and seashores. Each kind of watery place provides a habitat for some kind of plant life.

Among the many colorful flowers around ponds and rivers are the bright yellow marsh marigold and the purple loosestrife. While they prefer the shore, other plants root underwater, among them the water lily and many kinds of reeds and rushes. Several water plants do not root in soil at all, but simply float. Duckweeds and water hyacinths float on the surface, bladderworts just below it.

In bogs and swamps

Bogs are wet areas, usually with peaty soils that contain few nutrients. Typical vegetation includes mosses such as sphagnums, carnivorous plants like sundews and pitcher plants, and beautiful orchids in some places.

Wetlands with more fertile soil are generally called swamps or marshes. They support a wider range of flora than bogs, often including large trees such as the swamp

▲ Bladderwort floats in the water.

Q Its tiny bladders help it float. They also have another purpose. What is it?

cypress, which is also called the bald cypress. This grows abundantly in the many wetland regions in the southeastern United States, including the Great Cypress Swamp and the Everglades.

To support itself in the waterlogged soil, this tree grows huge buttresses around its base. It also sends up growths from its roots above the water-line, that help the roots "breathe."

In tropical and subtropical regions of the world, trees called mangroves grow on the margins where rivers meet the sea. They grow in the muddy sediment the rivers deposit in salty water. But they have adapted to their watery habitat by sending down roots from their trunks and branches down into the mud so that the roots are partly out of the water. And, like the swamp cypress, mangrove roots "breathe" directly in the air.

On the seashore

The seashore is another difficult habitat for plants because it is regularly covered and uncovered by salty sea water. Different kinds of grasses cover the salt-water marshes found along many seashores. Some grasses, such as eelgrass, even grow underwater.

Other plants besides grasses can tolerate the salty habitat. They include sea holly and the yellow horned poppy. One interesting plant is called glasswort because it was once used in glassmaking. When burned, its ashes contain soda, one of the ingredients in glass.

Q 1. What is the main ingredient in glass?

53

▲ The marsh marigold has flowers of a rich golden yellow color.

Q 2. The flowers are not what they seem. What is strange about them?

▲ Purple loosestrife carries a spike of flowers, which grow in rings around the stem.

▲ Mangrove trees grow in tropical and subtropical wetland regions, as here in the Florida Everglades. The trees send down roots from the branches, forming a dense impenetrable thicket.

Some Native Species at Risk

☆ **Monterey Cypress tree California**
Suffering from disease and coastal erosion.

☆ **Eureka Dune Grass, California**
Under threat by off-road vehicles like dune buggies.

☆ **Texas Wild Rice, Texas**
A water grass under threat because of commercial collecting, pollution, recreation.

☆ **North American Pawpaw tree, Florida**
Threatened by urban development.

☆ **Tennessee Green Pitcher plant, Tennessee**
Endangered by over-collecting and urban development.

☆ **Florida Arrowroot, Florida**
A rare cycad under threat because of resort expansion.

☆ **Arizona Agave, Arizona**
Threatened by over-collecting humans and by browsing animals.

☆ **Knowlton Cactus, New Mexico**
Endangered because of over-collecting and recreation.

Conserving our plants

The trees, wild flowers, and other plants that grace our land are part of our national heritage. But increasingly they are being threatened by our modern way of life.

Modern farming, for example, requires vast areas of land to grow crops and raise livestock. Over much of the country, the landscape is not natural, but manmade. Areas that were once meadows filled with native grasses and a profusion of wild flowers are now under the plow or are grazed by cattle and other livestock. Hedges that were once home to many species of plants and animals have also been rapidly disappearing. Many grasses that remain have had their wildlife decimated by agricultural sprays, used to keep crops healthy. Other vast tracts of land have been covered with highways, industrial parks, housing developments, and the like. In some places, mining activities are literally reshaping the landscape.

Such activities are bound to continue. So it is vital that we insure the least disturbance to our natural habitats. We must try to find alternatives to harmful practices, for example, using biological controls for killing pests instead of insecticides.

▶ A carpet of flowers planted alongside a highway in California. Such plantings not only beautify the environment, but also attract useful and attractive insects, such as bees and butterflies, and other wildlife.

On the positive side, our country is fortunate in having such a thriving national parks system, which looks after many of our most precious wild places and irreplaceable wildlife habitats. The national parks are in the forefront of the thrust toward a greater environmental awareness that will insure the preservation of our precious plant resources for future generations.

▲ All kinds of plants appear in this photograph, taken in Golden Gate Park, San Francisco. The lowliest ones are the lichens covering the rocks. Parks like this provide a welcome haven for plants in our big cities and often act as a lifeline for rare and endangered species.

Wildflower Center

To further your study of plants in general, and of native wild flowers in particular, write to the National Wildflower Research Center near Austin, Texas. (2600 FM 973 North Austin, Texas 78725. Telephone (512) 929 3600)

The Center was founded in 1982 by Lady Bird Johnson, wife of the former President of the United States, Lyndon B. Johnson. The purpose of this nonprofit organization is to become a catalyst to stimulate the preservation, propagation, and increased use of wildflowers and native plants throughout the United States.

The Center publishes a quarterly newsletter, "Wildflower," and will provide a list of companies from which you can buy the seeds of wildflowers.

Millions of Years Ago	Time Span	Details of Plant Life
2,500		A group of primitive cells called prokaryotes begins to harness the energy in sunlight to make food. This is the beginning of photosynthesis. Blue-green algae develop.
1,200		Cells develop a nucleus and become more complex. They are called eukaryotes.
Up to 590	PRECAMBRIAN	Only scant traces of life found in the rocks, such as structures called stromatolites, formed by algae.
590-248	PALEOZOIC ERA	The era of ancient life, divided into six periods.
590-505	Cambrian Period	An "explosion" of life occurs in the warm, shallow seas that covered the world in the form of different kinds of algae and seaweeds and a variety of simple plant-like animals, such as sponges and sea lilies.
504-438	Ordovician Period	Plant and animal life continue to flourish as the seas retreat and advance in turn.
437-408	Silurian Period	The first land plants appear near the end of the period.
407-360	Devonian Period	Plant life develops on land during this period. The first land plants are leafless and rootless. Then ferns develop, growing to considerable size. The land plants release oxygen into the atmosphere. The gradual buildup of oxygen lays the foundation for the emergence of air-breathing land animals.
359-286	Carboniferous Period	Land plants develop rapidly. Extensive forests of giant ferns and horsetails grow in warm, shallow swamps in many parts of the world. The first cone-bearing trees appear. When the forests die, decay, and are buried, they gradually change into coal.
285-248	Permian Period	Horsetails, seed ferns, and conifers continue to dominate plant life.
247-65	MESOZOIC ERA	The era of middle life, divided into three periods.
247-213	Triassic Period	Plants are relatively scarce at the beginning of the period, but are abundant by the end.
212-144	Jurassic Period	Huge forests of mainly ferns, horsetails, and conifers cover most of the land. They are inhabited by an increasing variety of "terrible lizards" – the dinosaurs.
143-65	Cretaceous Period	Many varieties of flowering plants develop, leading to the establishment of huge forests of broad-leaved trees. Also developing rapidly now are the ancestors of modern insects, feeding on the nectar the flowers produce. At the end of this period, many species of plants, along with the dinosaurs and other animals, are wiped out by a natural catastrophe.
64-Present Day	CENOZOIC ERA	The era of recent life, divided into two periods.
64-2	Tertiary Period	Many of today's most common plant families are established, such as the Compositae (daisy family), the Orchidaceae (orchid family), and the grasses. Plants begin to assume their present form.
2-Present Day	Quaternary Period	Repeated ice ages force the migration of plant (and animal) life. From about 10,000 years ago, human beings begin to influence the balance of nature by clearing forest land for agriculture and planting selected grasses (cereals) for food.

Glossary

ADAPTATION Features of a plant that make it fit in with its environment.

ALGAE (singular ALGA) The simplest and most primitive kind of plant, consisting of a single cell.

ANGIOSPERM A flowering plant that produces seeds inside a protective seed case.

ANNUAL A plant that lives for just one growing season. Peas and beans are examples.

ANNUAL RINGS See **GROWTH RINGS**.

ANTARCTIC The very cold region around the South Pole.

AQUATIC Living in the water.

ARCTIC The very cold region around the North Pole.

ASEXUAL REPRODUCTION Reproduction that does not depend on the coming together of male and female parts.

BIENNIAL A plant that takes two growing seasons to go through its life cycle. The foxglove is a biennial.

BIOLOGY The science of living things.

BOTANY The scientific study of plants.

BUDDING A method of reproduction in which a new organism grows as a bud on an existing plant and then separates. Yeast is an example.

CANOPY The upper layer of forest, formed by interlacing branches and leaves.

CAMBIUM A layer of cells in a woody plant, such as a tree, between the bark and the wood of the stem.

CARPEL The female part of a flowering plant that contains the ovary.

CARNIVOROUS PLANTS Those that eat animals, mainly insects.

58

CELL The smallest unit of a plant.

CEREALS Crops such as wheat, barley, and rice that bear their seeds as heads of grain. They belong to the grass family.

CHAPPARAL A large region of scrubland in California.

CHLOROPHYLL The green pigment in plants that harnesses the Sun's energy during photosynthesis.

CHLOROPLAST The part of a plant cell that contains chlorophyll.

CLIMBER A plant that climbs, such as ivy and bindweed.

COMPOSITE A flower head made up of hundreds of small flowers. Daisies are examples.

CONIFERS Trees that bear their seeds in cones. They are usually evergreen and have needle-like leaves.

CUTTING A piece cut from one plant that develops into another when planted.

DECIDUOUS TREES Trees that shed all their leaves at once, usually in the fall.

DESERT A region that has little if any rainfall during the year. Most deserts are very hot.

DICOTYLEDON A class of flowering plants whose seeds have two seed leaves. Roses and dandelions are examples.

DNA The substance in the nucleus of a cell that controls all cell functions. DNA is short for deoxyribonucleic acid.

EMBRYO A developing plant.

ENVIRONMENT The surroundings, including physical features, climate, and living things.

EPIPHYTE A plant that grows on another but makes its own food. Tropical orchids are examples. Contrast PARASITE.

EQUATOR An imaginary line around the Earth, midway between the North and South Poles.

EVERGREEN A plant that keeps its leaves all year long.

FERTILIZATION The coming together of male and female sex cells to create a new life.

FLORA Plant life.

GENUS The division in plant (or animal) classification above Species and below Family.

GERMINATION The period when a seed or spore begins to grow.

GRAFTING The adding of a piece of one plant to another.

GROWTH RINGS The rings you see when a tree trunk is cut down. Each ring represents a year's growth of wood.

GYMNOSPERM A plant that produces naked seeds; that is, seeds without a protective covering.

HABITAT The kind of surroundings in which a plant (or animal) lives.

HEARTWOOD The older, harder wood in the middle of a tree trunk that can no longer transport water up to the leaves. Contrast SAPWOOD.

HERBIVORES Animals that eat plants.

MANGROVES Trees that grow on the muddy shores of river deltas and estuaries in warm climates.

MARINE Living in the sea.

MONOCOTYLEDON A class of flowering plant whose seeds have just one seed leaf. Grasses and daffodils are examples.

OVARY The part of a plant in which the female sex cells are produced.

PAMPAS The temperate grassland regions in South America.

PARASITE A plant that lives on another and feeds on it, such as mistletoe. Contrast EPIPHYTE.

PERENNIAL A plant that lives for many growing seasons. All trees are perennials.

PHOTOSYNTHESIS The process by which plants manufacture their food.

PISTIL The female part of a flower, which develops into a seed when fertilized.

POLLEN The male cells of a flowering plant.

POLLINATION A process in which pollen is transferred from one flowering plant to another.

PRAIRIE The temperate grassland regions in North America.

RAIN FOREST Tropical and subtropical forest close to the equator, which receives plentiful rainfall all through the year.

REPRODUCTION An essential characteristic of living things: that an organism (plant or animal) can reproduce its own kind.

RESPIRATION The process by which living things (plants and animals) take in oxygen to "burn" their food and give out carbon dioxide as a waste product.

SAPWOOD The younger, softer wood in a tree trunk that transports water to the leaves. Contrast HEARTWOOD.

SAVANNA Tropical grassland, especially that in eastern and southern Africa.

SCRUB A hot, dry region with low, shrubby vegetation.

SEXUAL REPRODUCTION Reproduction brought about by the coming together of male and female parts.

SPECIES In general, species means kind. But more specifically, Species is the division in plant (and animal) classification below Genus. Scientifically, a plant (or an animal) is named by its genus and species. The scientific name for the common buttercup, for example, is Ranunculus acris, Ranunculus being the genus and acris the species.

SPORES Single-celled units that lower plants, such as fungi, produce during reproduction.

STAMEN The male part of a flower, which produces pollen.

STEPPE The temperate grassland regions of eastern Europe and Asia.

TEMPERATE CLIMATE A climate that is neither too hot nor too cold, and that has reasonable rainfall.

TRANSPIRATION The process in which plants give off excess water into the atmosphere in the form of water vapor.

TROPICS A region with a hot climate on either side of the Equator. Strictly speaking, it is the region between latitude $23\frac{1}{2}°$ North (the Tropic of Cancer) and latitude $23\frac{1}{2}°$ South (the Tropic of Capricorn).

TROPISM The movement of a plant in response to an external stimulus, such as light and gravity.

TUNDRA The very cold treeless wilderness in far northern regions of North America, Europe, and Asia.

UMBEL A flower head composed of a number of umbrella-shaped structures.

WETLANDS Regions where water lies on the surface most of the time, such as in esturies, mud flats, and swamps.

Answers

Page 6

Assuming your pencil to measure about 9/32 inch (7.5 mm) across, there would be about 1.2 million cells across the width. (Don't forget to allow for the area of the pencil lead in your calculations!)

Page 15

When you plunge the smoldering taper into the testtube, it should burst into flame again. This is because the gas inside the tube is oxygen, which is given out by plants as a waste product during photosynthesis.

Page 18

1. As the plant grows, more water needs to be taken in to support the food-making process going on in its leaves. Also, as it grows bigger, the plant needs firmer support. The larger roots satisfy both these needs.

2. The term "geotropism" refers to a plant bending because of gravity, from the Greek word geos, meaning Earth, as in geology, geography, and so forth. "Phototropism" refers to a plant bending because of light, from the Greek word photos, meaning light.

Investigation

When you put the jar on its side, the growing shoot and root will turn until they are growing vertically once more, the one growing upward, the other downward. And

▲ The willow herb produces tall spikes of pinkish-purple flowers. It is also called fireweed because it is one of the first plants to re-establish itself on land that has been burned.

▲ The harebell has slender stems bearing bluish-violet bell-shaped flowers. Sometimes called the Scottish bluebell, it is one of 300 species belonging to the bellflower family.

when you stand the jar upright again, the shoots will again bend until they are growing vertically.

Page 21

Strawberry plants can also reproduce like other flowering plants. The delicious fruits they bear contain seeds that will grow into new plants.

Page 23

These plants, called plantains, scatter their pollen in the wind.

Page 24

1. Grass pollen affects millions of people by causing hay fever.

2. When you shake a catkin, a cloud of pollen comes out.

Page 25

The bees that collect the pollen are the workers. They are females but they don't lay eggs or take part in reproduction. Only the true female, the queen, does this.

Page 28

Stinging nettle flowers are pollinated by the wind.

Page 29

When one species gains protection by resembling another, it is called mimicry.

Page 34

1. Seaweeds grow in relatively shallow waters because they need sunlight to make food by photosynthesis. The sea becomes darker the deeper you go.

2. By floating on the surface, the bladder wrack can get more sunlight than it could if it was submerged by the incoming tide.

Page 35

1. We find the remains of the ancient fern forests in the form of coal.

2. Mushrooms can't make their food by photosynthesis. They grow by extracting nourishment from decaying organic matter in the soil.

Page 39

Trees are perennials.

Page 48

Flowering plants are scarce on the forest floor because it is too dark. Fungi, however, abound because they don't need light and there is plenty of decaying organic matter for them to live on.

Page 52

The bladderwort also uses its bladders to trap insects. It is one of the carnivorous plants.

Page 53

1. The main ingredient in glass is sand. It is mixed with soda and lime and heated to high temperature in a furnace to make ordinary window glass, known as sodalime glass.

2 The yellow "petals" are not true petals. They are colored sepals.

For further reading

Cochrane.
Food Plants.
Steck-Vaughn, Austin, TX. 1991.

Jennings, Terry.
Seeds and Seedlings.
Childrens Press, Chicago, IL. 1989.

Landau, Elaine.
Endangered Plants.
Franklin Watts, New York. 1992.

Madgwick, Wendy.
Flowering Plants.
Steck-Vaughn, Austin, TX. 1990.

Maurice, Bleifield.
Botany Projects for Young Scientists.
Childrens Press, Chicago, IL. 1992.

Nielson, Nancy.
Carnivorous Plants.
Franklin Watts, New York. 1992.

Rainis, Kenneth.
Nature Projects for Young Scientists.
Franklin Watts, New York. 1989.

Sabin, Louis.
Plants, Seeds, and Flowers.
Troll, 1985.

Suzuki, David.
Looking at Plants.
Wiley, Chicago, IL. 1992.

Wiessinger, John.
Flowers, Ferns, and Fungi – Right Before Your Eyes.
Enslow, Hillside, NJ. 1989.

Index

(Numbers in *italics* refer to illustrations)